The Thrang Coun
Mallerstang, Kirkby St

Many names around this dale come from the Vikings, who settled here a thousand years ago. 'The Thrang' means a busy place - but it offers peace for those who come to relax and unwind, surrounded by the dramatic, unspoilt scenery of Mallerstang. The house was built in the 1830s by the Vicar, and his influence can be seen in the stained glass windows, the spire, and imposing gothic front doors. Outside it may look a bit solemn, but there is a warm welcome. (Several have remarked that it is like being at home - but without the washing up)!

We have been awarded the RAC's 'Highly Acclaimed' classification, and have had complimentary comments in 'The Sunday Times', 'Washington Post', and 'Country Walking'. We are delighted that two thirds of our bookings are guests who return, or from recommendations. With 6 comfortable, en-suite bedrooms, you can be sure of personal attention. (We are also just the right size to be 'taken over' by groups - for a walking weekend, or for a family celebration).

Our five course candle-lit dinners are much appreciated. (Many guests ask for the recipes of, for example, our Parsnip and Apple Soup or Sticky Toffee Pudding, so we are producing a 'Thrang Cook Book' to join our booklet of Local Walks). We prepare all dishes freshly, so meals should be booked in advance by non-residents. We are happy to cater for Vegetarian or other diets, (eg gluten free), but need to know of any special requirements before we start cooking.

Good Aga-cooked food, a friendly atmosphere, and the character of the house all contribute to a memorable visit, but we must admit that nature plays a large part, too. Mallerstang has been described as 'almost a state secret'. There is a feeling of timelessness, and you are almost surprised if you meet another wall ...quiet paths beside the River Eden, or on the fell tops.

The cliff face of Mallerstang Edge dominates one side of the dale, and the rocky profile of Wild Boar Fell rears up behind us. A hundred yards away the old Highway crosses the present road. This is sometimes called Lady Anne Clifford's Way - in memory of the indomitable Countess of Westmoreland who often travelled along this track 400 years ago.

One of Lady Anne's favourite places was Pendragon Castle. This is now a ruin, but it has a magnificent setting and a feeling of mystery. It is said that it was originally built by King Arthur's father, Uther Pendragon. Another owner was Sir Hugh de Morville, one of the four knights who murdered St Thomas a Beckett in Canterbury Cathedral. (If you look towards Wild Boar Fell from near the castle, you can see a profile of the Archbishop - a sight which haunted Sir Hugh). Reminders of even more ancient times, Bronze Age burial mounds, known as 'Giants Graves', can be seen beside the river at Birkett Common.

The Highway has been discovered by more walkers in recent years. Many travel on the Settle to Carlisle line to Garsdale, then walk through Mallerstang, re-joining the train at Kirkby Stephen. Our licensed Tea Room in the old Coach House makes a welcome stop along the way. (Even when we are closed, we always try to open up for walkers).

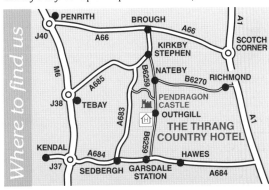

Where to find us

For further information, contact:

THE THRANG COUNTRY HOTEL,
MALLERSTANG,
KIRKBY STEPHEN,
CUMBRIA, CA17 4JX
TEL: 07683 71889

The Green Dragon
Hardraw, Hawes

The Green Dragon is a gem; and I warrant that, having sampled its delights never again will the name invoke a mother-in-law image!

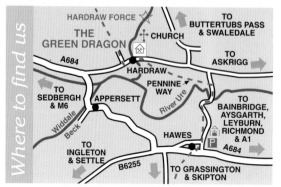

It nestles snugly into the lower folds of Stags Fell, warm and secure, occupying a site that has held an inn for 700 years. The present hostelry has been skilfully and tastefully extended in recent years to provide very comfortable accommodation indeed. Its stout walls enclose 16 bedrooms, each with its own en suite facilities and colour TV. There is about it a welcoming air, making it ideally suited as a well appointed refuge for discerning people in need of a break from the hurly-burly of city life.

Hikers and sightseers alike are drawn to the Green Dragon like bears to a honey pot at the heel of an action packed day because they know that that's the time to become immersed in an ambience of peace, serenity and bonhomie, richly garnished with mouth watering fare and a jar or two of 'falling about fluid' or a drop of the hard stuff or both, all of which the Green Dragon provides in full measure with consummate ease.

Ever had the feeling that an exciting expedition into beautiful country is the bees knees but that the inn you are staying at is so laid back, so comfy, you simply can't be bothered to make the effort? Well, at the Green Dragon there is no such problem. This lucky inn owns several acres of wonderful dales country and has within its grounds Hardraw Force, Britain's highest above ground, single drop waterfall. Like a slim veil the fall drops into a natural, wooded amphitheatre where, in mid-summer, wagtails and dippers flitter and the dawn chorus sets the place chirruping at the sheer joy of it all.

The foot of Hardraw Scar is a natural amphitheatre with acoustic properties of so high a standard that each September it becomes the venue for the famous Hardraw Brass Band contest, which attracts enthusiasts in their droves, many with their Nikons in their hands.

The Green Dragon provides a balance of peace and quiet with civilized facilities, making it an ideal spot for absolutely anyone...not only for individuals and families, but for corporate groups too. If you have a management team in need of seclusion, this is the place. Facilities can be made available for meeting rooms, communications, audio-visual and other business equipment; and John and Pauline Stead promise you won't be disturbed!

From its ancient beams, its log fires and the hospitality of mine hosts to the friendliness the locals habitually extend to the visitors, the place exudes its genuineness. Meals served in the fine dining hall always include a choice between good Yorkshire traditionalism and continental sophistication; and bar meals are also available.

If you prefer to look after yourself, five self-catering apartments are available; with company and a meal you don't have to cook just twenty yards away. Lovers of real ale will appreciate the range on offer in the bar, where is found the inn's only peculiarity. It is old and Theakstons brew it.

THE YORKSHIRE DALES
Green Dales & Purple Moors

Introduction

The Yorkshire Dales cover an area of 680 square miles, most of which lie in the Yorkshire Dales National Park, which was created in 1954 and for some reason did not include Nidderdale, which has now been declared an Area of Outstanding Natural Beauty. The dales can be counted by the hundred, the main ones being Swaledale, Wensleydale, Wharfedale, Ribblesdale, Nidderdale, Arkengarthdale, Airedale, Colsterdale, Coverdale, Littondale, Malhamdale, Garsdale and Dentdale.

The topography of the larger dales is as diverse as the direction of flow of the rivers they contain. Most run eastwards, others westerly, and some favour a southerly route.

Where Swaledale is wild, steep sided and narrow, its neighbour, Wensleydale, is broad and well wooded; where Wharfedale is long and winding, Ribblesdale comprises rolling moorland between mountainous peaks. That is the way of it: each dale differing to a greater or lesser degree from the others, each one offering a refreshingly different charm.

The one thing they all have in common is a farming tradition that stems from the Stone Age. Farming began in the dales during the Neolithic period and by the C12th monastic estates and hunting forests covered most of the area. Following the Dissolution of 1536-9, the great abbey estates and granges were sold, the gentry and London merchants being the first to acquire freeholds. Later, sitting tenants obtained freeholds and a new class of yeoman farmer came into being.

It was during the years between 1630 and 1730 that most of the dales' farmhouses were built, or older ones rebuilt. Field houses sprang up throughout this valley and incised Pennine upland, particularly in Swaledale where almost every field had one.

Until 1870 much of the land was common grazing ground with only the irregular shaped fields of the valley bottoms being enclosed with dry stone walls. Then, as over the next forty years the walls, now dividing the land more regularly like a chequer-board, enclosed previous common land, many small farms fell foul of the system and larger farms swallowed them. It was a time of great hardship among many whose main livelihood came from the land.

The very texture of today's dales' landscape, the very rhythm of its rural lifestyle, is determined by farming which remains the quintessence of the dales' scene. Of this, sheep farming remains the central pivot and the Yorkshire Dales National Park emblem, the head of a Swaledale tup, acknowledges this fact.

The sturdy Swaledales graze in huge flocks throughout the year on the wild and lonely, higher slopes of Swaledale and other northern dales. Their wool, which is too coarse for knitting, but ideally suited for carpet making, was the foundation of the dales' prosperity.

Dalesbred sheep are more common in the southern dales while in the western dales the rough fell sheep predominate.

Large areas of dales' moorland, a purple sea in the Autumn, are preserved because they are home to the red grouse; and lucrative grouse shooting rights are a boon to the local economy.

All in all, there is no part of the Pennines so rich in natural beauty, so well laced with English history as the Yorkshire Dales, whose farming tradition is king.

Purple moors above Swaledale

The Sportsman's Arms Hotel
Wath-in-Nidderdale

Wath-in-Nidderdale lies in quiet seclusion in surroundings of unusual charm through which the River Nidd winds its way. It is located within a convenient quarter mile of Gouthwaite Reservoir, which is famous among ornithologists for the wealth of its bird life. The Sportsman's Arms Restaurant and Hotel is sited in this lovely spot and has a reputation for warmth and friendliness. This ensures that visitors will have a relaxed and pleasant stay, winter and summer alike.

Dating from the C17th, the hotel is set in its own grounds with magnificent views of the surrounding Nidderdale countryside. Only 35 miles from York, 16 from Harrogate and even less from Ripon, it is ideally placed as a base from which to explore the exciting, Yorkshire Dales with their wealth of beautiful scenery.

Culture vultures are spoiled rotten: cast your eyes on this little lot of interesting places to visit from The Sportsman's Arms. It is a formidable list: York Minister: Ripon Cathedral: Fountains Abbey: Bolton Abbey: Jervaulx, Rievaulx and Byland Abbeys: Fountains Hall: Harewood House and Newby Hall: Skipton, Middleham, Bolton, Ripley, Richmond and Knaresborough Castles: Brimham Rocks and Stump Cross Caverns. Whichever you choose can be visited at leisure and still allow you time to return for your evening meal.

For dinner there is the choice of the a la carte menu or the prix fixe menu at £19.75, which includes half a bottle of wine per person. For residents staying two or more nights the table d'hote meal is £13.50; and all the prices include VAT.

There is an extensive choice of wines from the 170 bins in the wine cellar.

A speciality of The Sportsman's Arms Hotel is fresh seafood with grouse, pheasant and venison in season. All the food is fresh, no frozen food being used, and no chips are served. Lunches and evening meals are served in the bar, the restaurant being used for evening meals and Sunday Lunches only.

The Sportsman's Arms Hotel is listed in all the major food guides.

Set in its own pleasant grounds, The Sportsman's Arms is tastefully decorated throughout. There are eight comfortable bedrooms, three lounges and a public bar. The restaurant is fully licenced; and during the winter months open fires spread cheer and warmth, enhancing the hotels friendliness.

Ray and Jane Carter are the proprietors. Ray does the cooking, ably assisted by Chris, Dean and Penny while Veronica and Victoria run the front of the house as they have done for the past twelve years.

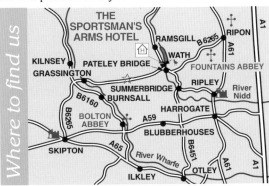

Nidd is a Celtic word, meaning 'shining'. The river has its genesis among the heights of Great and Little Whernside and Great Haw. Its dale is a fairly long one and is mostly carved through Millstone Grit. Much of its water, held in dams, supplies, among other places, Bradford.

Wath, which means 'crossing place of a river', has had no new buildings since the 1890s, not even a lamp post. It is totally unspoilt, which is more than can be said of yourself if you stay at The Sportsman's Arms Hotel.

For further information, contact:

**THE SPORTSMAN'S ARMS HOTEL,
WATH-IN-NIDDERDALE,
PATELEY BRIDGE, NR HARROGATE,
NORTH YORKSHIRE, HG3 5PP
TEL: 0423 711306**

Cockett's Hotel & Restaurant
Hawes

If you are seeking a C17th, stone built hotel which, while retaining its old world charm, provides all the modern facilities you would expect of an English Tourist Board registered auberge, and if it has to be in beautiful Wensleydale, then Cockett's Hotel and Restaurant, in Hawes, is for you.

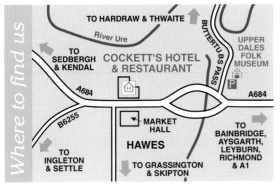

Hawes, one of the highest market towns in England, stands sentinel at one end of the famous Buttertubs Pass with tiny hamlets gathered about it like chicks around a clucking hen. It houses an excellent Folk Museum filled with antiquities from the Upper Dales, lovingly collected over many years by Joan Ingilby and Marie Hartley, authors of many books on life and traditions in the dales. It is home to the renowned Wensleydale cheeses, has a rope works two centuries old where visitors are welcome to inspect its traditional techniques and an imposing market hall where more than 100,000 sheep and lambs and 12,000 cattle are sold every year. It is ideally placed for exploring all those romantic places associated with James Herriot's memorable characters; and this is where, for true romantics, the years roll back and the love affair with this glorious landscape begins. Here, heart throbbing at the thrill of it all, fantasy becomes reality.

'Eh! Mabel, just look at yone hillside! That's where Herriot slid on a cow pat and all the cows started clapping'. Such magical moments come rarely, but Upper Wensleydale can provide them.

There are eight letting bedrooms at Cockett's two with four poster beds so why not wear a nightcap and pretend you are Old Rowley? It should be fun and is certainly different. There are six en suite bedrooms and the hotel has full central heating. Both full board and B & B are on offer and for winter and spring breaks three nights can be had for the price of two.

The cosy bar is purpose built for relaxation. There, companionable quaffing from a wide range of beers and spirits or from a list of more than 60 wines will put a smile on your day.

Children over ten are welcome to the hotel and the restaurant is open to non-residents but, sorry, no dogs.

Fred and Mary Bedford, who bought Cockett's in 1990 have made the following pledge to their guests: 'When you arrive only you can decide if our accommodation entices you to stay. When you leave only you can decide whether our hospitality entices you to return. Our Hotel cannot live and grow unless you return and we therefore pledge to do everything possible to make your stay an enjoyable one'.

They are fulfilling that pledge admirably. Three and five course dinners are served throughout the year, except Sundays, and the Table d'Hote menu is changed daily. Lunches are served from Easter until November, except Tuesdays, and as befits an establishment smothered with awards and recommendations, the fare is fabulous. It is the proprietors' desire to provide English and French cooking of the highest standard at a reasonable price. Be it 'Fillet Steak filled with Stilton' or 'Medallions of Venison Ardenaise' the choice is yours. English or French.

For further information, contact:

**COCKETT'S HOTEL & RESTAURANT,
MARKET PLACE, HAWES,
NORTH YORKSHIRE, DL8 3RD
TEL: 0969 667312
FAX: 0969 667162**

Falls Country Club
Aysgarth

'Large or small, we serve them all' is not the Falls Country Club motto; but a more descriptive one would be difficult to find because that is precisely what this enterprising club sets out to do. Furthermore, it succeeds because it offers quality catering at an affordable price. The service is as friendly as only a caring family-run business can make it; and this is reflected in its fast-growing reputation for good fare among travellers from far and wide.

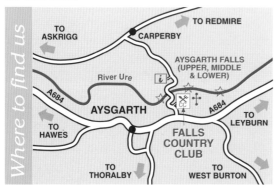

Where to find us

Until 1989, when it was purchased by the present owners, the Falls Country Club was called the Falls Motel. Since then it has been refurbished throughout, and it shows.

The dining room is spacious with a seating capacity of over 100, and this, combined with a well equipped self-service cafeteria, ensures that large and small parties can be served with anything from a cup of tea to a full meal.

Coach parties are always welcome in the self-service cafe and menus for the dining room are available on request. The dining room is as light and airy as the Yorkshire puddings served there, and both rooms are licenced.

The brew is local, comes from Masham and goes down a treat. It helps to lubricate the many social occasions held there by the local community, the dinner dances and the wedding receptions.

It is particularly convenient for wedding receptions because Aysgarth's historic parish church is nearby and it is there that so many of the local matches are made. The church is a large one, well sited on the same hillside as the Falls Country Club. It has on show a wonderful display of marquetry that was rescued from Jervaulx Abbey by monks at the Dissolution and rehoused there.

The River Ure, which skirts the hillside on which the Falls Country Club rests, is at its most dramatic here as it plunges over the magnificent Aysgarth Falls, the centrepiece of a renowned beauty spot. The Falls were recently featured in the Warner Brother's blockbuster 'Robin Hood, Prince of Thieves', which was mediaeval history as it might have been; and the mill below the higher falls supplied six hundred dozen jerseys to Garibaldi's Army of Unification.

Yorkshire's only genuine lake, Semer Water, is only a short car ride away. It was born in the Ice Age when a huge glacier, spread across the Vale of York, prevented movement by the Wensleydale glacier which, in turn, blocked the flow of ice from Raydale so that, when the ice melted, drift blocked the foot of the valley forming a large lake. Eventually water cut through the drift, forming the River Bain, England's shortest, and reducing the size of the lake considerably.

Many visitors to Wensleydale, attracted by fine natural features like these, are forever on the lookout for somewhere in which to relax over a meal, a snack or a drink, a place in which to relax while reminiscing about the day's adventures. The Falls Country Club fulfills that need; and does so admirably.

For further information, contact:

**FALLS COUNTRY CLUB,
AYSGARTH, NR LEYBURN,
WENSLEYDALE,
NORTH YORKSHIRE, DL8 3SR
TEL: 0969 663232**

Muker Store & Tea Shop
Muker

In 1740 the Church of England had a vicarage built in Muker and today tea and sympathy are still dispensed there; only nowadays the setting is more secular. Food for thought has become thought for food. However, as befits an establishment with an ecclesiastical genesis, the first is last and the last is first. It all depends on the direction of approach.

For many glorious years this proud distinction was held by a renowned inn, the Cat Hole at Keld. It was the first, or the last hostelry in Swaledale and famed for the excellence of its home-made refections. Cat Hole ham and eggs were famed throughout Christendom.

Then it changed hands, and unfortunately its licence was not renewed, it was no longer a welcoming haven for cyclists and hikers, it closed its doors, turned its back on this world, its eyes on the next one, and a miracle happened. The honest, hard working, God fearing dalesfolk, noted for their fair minded approach to life, did the unthinkable. They became angry, lost their tempers, raised merry hell; but to no avail.

Happily, all was not lost, for at Muker David and Gwen May had established a tea room which was now the uppermost one in Swaledale, and Stuart May was managing their General Store.

Muker is 17 miles west of Richmond and the store, the only one in Muker, is the last one in Swaledale. So the Mays have pulled off a 'spring double', and the beneficiaries are the very visitors rejected when the Cat Hole changed hands.

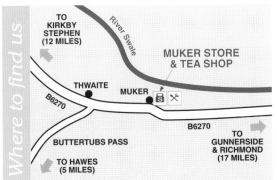

This is a wild land, bounded by high, untrammelled fells from where peaty becks plunge in plumes of milky white spray from craggy fastnesses and breath-taking views abound at every turn.

It is a tough environment, laced with dry stone walls and threaded with exciting paths that test the metal of creaking limbs. It is Gods country and the beautiful Swale is at its heart.

Muker Store and Tea Shop is a welcome refuge at the end of a long day's hike in the dales. Its Yorkshire rarebit, savoury cheese mixed with beer and served with gammon ham goes down a treat. Gwen's beef and kidney pie is simply delicious and if you haven't sampled her Theakston's Old Peculiar cake served with Swaledale cheese there's a treat in store.

In the two delightful tea rooms, which seat 30 and on the small south-facing patio, which seats 12, morning coffee, lunches and afternoon teas, hot meals and cold, are served until 5pm.

The tea shop is open from 10.30am until 5pm from Easter until 1st November every day except Wednesday and Thursday. From November to Easter it is weekends only, but, oh what weekends.

A succinct apocryphal tale says it all. Two Russian peasants were looking at the sun.

'Look', said one. 'The sun is smiling'.

'Because it is looking at the motherland?' the other suggested.

'No', the first peasant replied. 'The sun smiles because it knows that before the day is over it will be at Muker Tea Shop'.

For further information, contact:

**MUKER STORE & TEA SHOP,
MUKER, RICHMOND,
NORTH YORKSHIRE,
DL11 6QG
TEL: 0748 86409**

Palmer Flatt Hotel
Aysgarth

As villages go, Aysgarth has the edge on most for age. It was around some 1800 years before Christ, only it didn't answer to that name in those days. It was mentioned in the Domesday Book as being held by Gorfried and was valued at eight shillings. At that time it was called Eschescard. Nowadays, it is a place of great renown, largely because of the magnificent set of three limestone ledges over which the River Ure spills, frequently in a turmoil of frothy spume, as it flows below the village. Everybody has heard of Aysgarth Falls: even people who have not heard of Wensleydale have heard of them. I wish I knew the name of their PR man! Even the film makers have heard of Aysgarth Falls. Recently a famous production company shot scenes for 'Robin Hood - Prince of Thieves' on the Falls and now many people think they are in Sherwood Forest. But, of course they aren't as anyone in Palmer Flatt Hotel will tell you.

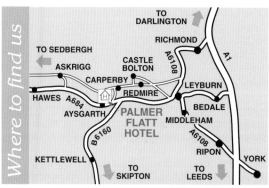

This fine building stands on the right hand corner of the steep road from the Ure where it joins the Hawes to Leyburn road, one of two main arteries that thread the valley, one on either side of the Ure.

Way back in 1594 this steep road crossed the river on a nine feet wide packhorse bridge, passing an old corn mill with a chequered history before tackling the steep valley side to the Palmer Flatt Hotel which, in those days, was a coaching inn. There, well lathered, the horses were fed, watered and stabled, as they had been ever since the days of the Crusades against the Moslems. For, since those times, a hospice has stood on this site; and it was pilgrims returning from the Holy Land bearing palm branches that gave Palmer Flatt its name.

Legend has it that a tunnel from the hotel's cellar joins it to Aysgarth's magnificent church, which, because of its size, is known as the Cathedral of the Dales. Once, determined folk, carrying candles searched the cellar for tell-tale draughts, but none were found. However, times change and today Palmer Flatt Hotel has draughts galore: draught real ale: draught Yorkshire: draught John Smiths: draught guest beers. For company they have Carlsberg and Coors lagers and, to remind folk of peaty becks, draught Guinness. For those allergic to draughts there is a large selection of spirits.

The bar and restaurant are spacious; and children are welcomed to the hotel which has ten fully en-suite bedrooms, some with four-poster beds and all with tea and coffee-making facilities, colour TVs and telephones.

It's enough to make a good, Christian pilgrim slap his palms in despair! He never had bar snacks, an a la carte Restaurant, a desert with an extra 's', and traditional Sunday Lunch. He never attended wedding receptions or large parties, all of which are available today at the Palmer Flatt Hotel, where fresh meat and vegetables are supplied daily to create mouth-watering home-made meals.

The Palmer Flatt is 'The' House in Aysgarth and in 'The' house the visitor's considerations are always noted by Hansard. For it is Val Hansard and her family who run this fine establishment for the benefit of all.

For further information, contact:

**PALMER FLATT HOTEL,
AYSGARTH, LEYBURN,
NORTH YORKSHIRE, DL8 3SR
TEL: 0969 663228
FAX: 0969 663182**

The Friar's Head
Akebar Park, Wensleydale

It is common knowledge that Wensleydale is famous for its Kings and Queens, castles and abbeys, waterfalls, its purple heather moors, race-horses, little white lambs, golden corn, green fields, real ale and cheese. Everyone knows that it is an area of outstanding beauty, magnificent views and excellent walking.

Fewer people are aware that its best kept secret lies just inside Akebar Caravan Park entrance, alongside the A684, an equidistant five miles from Leyburn and Bedale.

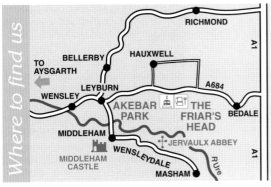

Those who are aware and enjoy an occupational walk can play croquet or bowls in front of The Friar's Head before or after they dine. On the adjacent golf course families can choose to play either nine or eighteen holes in accordance with their skill and ability or test out their golfing ambitions on the covered driving range which is opening in the summer. All are on a 'pay and play' basis and clubs and bowls may be hired.

There is a point on the course at which fine views of two National Parks and the Vale of York can be obtained and the stream which meanders through the course was made magical by Badger, Ratty, Mole and their friends in Kenneth Graham's 'Wind in the Willows'.

Wensleydale's best kept secret, however, is a pub and restaurant called The Friar's Head. "We had no idea it was here" is a frequent comment to the pub's owners, Colin and Joyce Ellwood. Yet it is old enough to have been part of a Jervaulx Abbey Grange. In 1826 at the time of the highway murder, which is recorded on the nearby Murder Stone, inscribed with the chilling words "DO NO MURDER", the old building was a tavern owned by Sally Humphries. Her involvement is recorded in the York newspaper of the day reporting the trial. The

welcome today is as warm as the log fire crackling in the hearth and the pastoral view from the conservatory and terrace takes first time visitors by surprise.

Linda and Neville Lloyd, who manage the fully licenced pub, have a reputation for keeping and serving traditional ales and interesting wines, some with their own labels. These are much appreciated, as is the expertise of Head Chef Stephen Ross, whose tasty dishes are influenced by daily availability of local produce. Everything is cooked to order and only the freshest ingredients are used. The menus are imaginative, full of flavour and don't cost the earth. Super value!

Lunches are served seven days a week from noon until 2pm and evening meals are available from 6pm on weekdays and 7pm on Sundays; and, yes, it is advisable to book evening meals at peak times.

Meals are served either in the main bar or the luxuriant conservatory, appropriately called The Cloisters, which has a flagged floor, can seat seventy and is centred by two giant stone slab tables strong enough to withstand the weight of spontaneous dancing at private parties!

Your visit to The Friar's Head could easily become a habit!

For further information, contact:

**THE FRIAR'S HEAD,
AKEBAR PARK, WENSLEYDALE,
NORTH YORKSHIRE,
DL8 5LY
TEL: 0677 450201**

The Red Lion Inn
Langthwaite, Arkengarthdale

Langthwaite, situated almost half way up Arkengarthdale, the most northerly dale in Yorkshire, is on the eastern bank of Arkle Beck whereas the narrow road that threads the dale keeps to its western side. The tiny hamlet is approached over a lovely hump-back-bridge and thereby hangs a happy tale of serendipity for traffic bypasses this cluster of buildings snuggled around a central square, allowing it to retain its flavour of yesteryear when transport was only one horse power, life, though hard, was in accord with the seasons and people had time for one another.

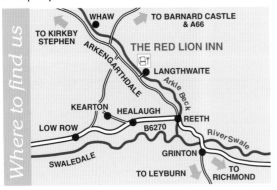

Again by happy chance, Disney Productions used it in 'Escape From The Dark', since when Langthwaite has been used frequently both in large screen productions and TV films like 'A Woman of Substance', 'All Creatures Great and Small', 'Hold The Dream', 'Andy Robson', 'Century Falls' and 'Dales Dairy'.

Langthwaite's C17th Red Lion Inn became a focal point for the film crews and its beamed ceilings, tiny snug and cosy bar have been the setting for many a silver screen, and TV film. Many of the famous actors and actresses were so impressed with the inn's pervasive, relaxed, cheerful atmosphere that they keep returning simply for the pleasure of it.

Inside the Red Lion, either in the main bar, the snug to the side of it, to which children are allowed at lunchtime or outside should you prefer it, morning coffee, bar snacks and bar meals are served and fine food it is, too! I've tried it many times and keep going back for more; and no, I am not a glutton for punishment: It really is a pleasure. With casseroles, various quiches, pizzas and curries, salads, ploughman's lunches with pate or cheese, toasted sandwiches and a good selection of sweets you are spoiled for choice.

Food is available every lunchtime from 12 noon until 2 o'clock, soup and toasted sandwiches are served until 2.30pm and tea and coffee during opening hours.

Evenings are devoted to the serious business of drinking, so no evening meals are served to cause distraction. For enjoyable drinking a good 'crack' is the finest adjunct to hand-pulled John Smith's Bitter, Theakston's XB and Bitter, Black Sheep Bitter, Murphy's Stout and Carlsberg Lager. Spirits are there for those who like something to chase and have not heard of girls. The licencee, Mrs Rowena Hutchinson keeps a good supply of minerals for whoever is driving.

In the C16th, the expression 'Red Lion Lane' was used jokingly to refer to the throat. So it is appropriate that convivial evenings at the Red Lion are devoted to lubricating that thoroughfare.

The red lion was both the badge of John of Gaunt and a heraldic reference to Scotland. When James VI of Scotland became James I of England he diplomatically ordered that the red lion should be displayed in public places. There are at least 600 pubs called the Red Lion, so make sure you go to the right one, the Red Lion Inn, Langthwaite.

The New Inn
Clapham, near Settle

The New Inn, a former coaching inn, which was built in 1776, has provided a welcome stop for travellers to the Lake District and Scotland since the C18th. Visitors to the Yorkshire Dales stay there frequently.

Keith and Barbara Mannion, who purchased The New Inn in 1987 have had the hotel extensively and sympathetically altered over the past six years. All the rooms are en suite and there is a resident's lounge on the first floor. Both were trained in catering at Skipton college and Andrew, the chef, who was trained at Morecambe and Lancaster college, has been at The New Inn for twelve years. So the high standard of catering is well established. The hotel is substantial and roomy. The main bar seats 50, the lounge bar 28, and the pool games area a further 12. There is seating for 66 in the restaurant, the resident's lounge seats 16, the beer garden 36 and at the front of the hotel the seating is 22 with riverside seating for 26.

The facilities are excellent, with breakfast, morning coffee, bar meals, lunch and evening meals and afternoon teas daily. There is a choice of table d'hote or a la carte menus and traditional lunch is served every Sunday. Whether you want a meal in one of the bars or to eat in the restaurant, the resident chef will satisfy your requirements. Pheasant in red wine and trout are among the tasteful dishes served in the restaurant. Home-made dishes include vegetarian fare like spicey bean casserole and cheese and leek pie. Or there is beef and beer cottage pie, game casserole, lasagne or curries.

The restaurant is open from 7pm until 9.30pm. The bar, which is open from 11.30am until 3pm weekdays, serves meals from 12 noon until about 2pm. On Saturdays serving is from 11am until 11pm and on Sundays between 12 noon and 3pm and from 7pm until 10.30pm.

There is a good selection of beers, including Dent, Tetleys, McEwans 80/-, Youngers Number 3, and John Smiths. Fosters and Carlsberg lagers are also on tap. Bottled beer is served, as are Britvic soft drinks. Tea and coffee are also available.

The Restaurant and Cocktail Bar are available for wedding receptions, business meetings and private parties. The wonderful countryside that surrounds The New Inn makes a dramatic difference to the success of business get-togethers. You will relish an atmosphere that is refreshing and relaxing and very, very friendly, with the personal service of the residential proprietors.

The New Inn is sited in Clapham, which is an ideal centre for your exploration of the magnificent Yorkshire Dales. Or you can fish for trout in the hotel's own river, shoot game in season, play golf or ride at nearby centres. Then there are the Three Peaks of Ingleborough, Whernside and Pen-y-ghent just waiting to be climbed and the Gaping Gill cave system worthy of exploration.

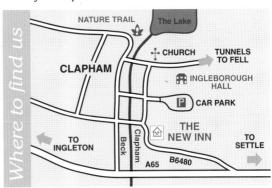

Michael Faraday was born in Clapham, which is where the Victorian botanist, Reginald Farrer, father of the English rock garden, had his home.

The New Inn is in good company.

For further information, contact:

**THE NEW INN,
CLAPHAM, NR SETTLE,
VIA LANCASTER,
NORTH YORKSHIRE, LA2 8HH
TEL: 05242 51203 FAX: 05242 51496**

Walk 1 - Ingleton's Waterfall Wonderland

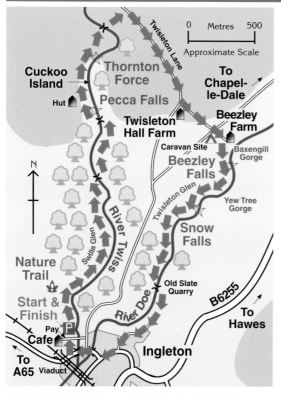

Cuckoo Island

Hut

Thornton Force

To Chapel-le-Dale

Twisleton Lane

Pecca Falls

Twisleton Hall Farm

Beezley Farm

Caravan Site

Baxengill Gorge

Beezley Falls

N

Twisleton Glen

Yew Tree Gorge

River Twiss

Swilla Glen

Snow Falls

Nature Trail

Old Slate Quarry

B6255

Start & Finish

Pay P

Cafe

River Doe

To Hawes

To A65 Viaduct

Ingleton

0 Metres 500

Approximate Scale

Distance: 4.5 Miles (7.2 km)

From the car park near Ingleton viaduct take a clear path along the west side of the Twiss, the Doe on some maps, up Swilla Glen Gorge, crossing to the east bank after a mile.

Continue upstream to re-cross at Pecca Falls, beyond where steps are laid at awkward places, eventually leading out of the gorge, beyond where Thornton Force is reached. A little further on cross the stream, climb a stepped path and cross a field to a lane.

Turn right, along it, past Twisleton Hall Farm, cross a stile at a gate, descend a field, cross a lane, passing a caravan site, to reach Beezley Farm.

Go right, fronting it, descend, following pointers, to Beezley Falls on the River Doe, the Greta on some maps, and take the stepped path downstream past spectacular Baxengill Gorge, Yew Tree Gorge and Snow Falls in Twisleton Glen.

Cross the gorge on a footbridge and follow a signposted path to Ingleton, continuing downhill, between buildings, to recross the Doe and return to the start.

A small fee is paid at the car park; but nevertheless, this walk is an absolute bargain!

Walk 2 - How Stean Gorge Circular

Distance: 1.5 Miles (2.4 km)

From How Stean car park cross the gorge and immediately turn right along the gorge walk, at first alongside the spectacular water course, then curving left, away from it, soon to nudge the Stean to Lofthouse road. Here leave the path and continue westwards, towards Stean, along the road.

The hamlet has neither church nor pub nor shop to disturb the serenity of the surrounding countryside; and it is there that the road you are on ends. On approaching Stean, short of where the road curves left turn right, as signposted, and follow a delightful path across fields, clearly waymarked, to Middlesmoor where St Chad's Church is well worth a visit and from where the view up and down the dale will take your breath away.

From the outskirts of Middlesmoor turn right along a quiet road, descending, steeply at one point to a T-junction. Turn right, pass a coach park and re-cross How Stean Beck.

Opposite How Stean Cottage go right along the gorge walk, past the two footbridges over the gorge, which you can cross if you like, to the car park from where Cat Hole and Tom Taylor's Cave await your inspection.

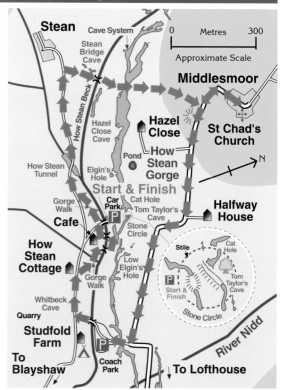

Stean

Cave System

Stean Bridge Cave

Middlesmoor

How Stean Beck

Hazel Close Cave

Hazel Close

St Chad's Church

How Stean Tunnel

Pond

Elgin's Hole

How Stean Gorge

N

Start & Finish

Gorge Walk

Car Park

Cat Hole

Tom Taylor's Cave

Halfway House

Cafe

Stone Circle

How Stean Cottage

Low Elgin's Hole

Gorge Walk

Whitbeck Cave

Quarry

Studfold Farm

To Blayshaw

Coach Park

To Lofthouse

Stile

Cat Hole

P

Start & Finish

Tom Taylor's Cave

Stone Circle

River Nidd

0 Metres 300

Approximate Scale

Walk 3 - A Winder Wonderland

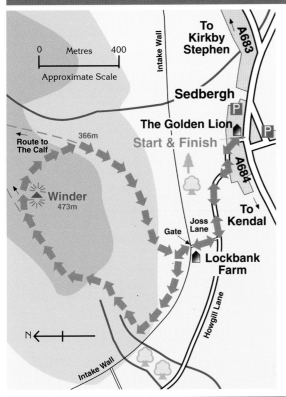

Distance: **3 Miles (4.8 km)**

Sedbergh and Winder have close links. The school song is called 'Winder' and memories of tough runs up its steep sides usually remain with the school's old boys throughout their lives. Winder helps to build character, to turn a boy into a man. A walk up it is certainly a challenge and you may become a better person for the experience.

Leave Sedbergh's main street at The Golden Lion, uphill, along Howgill Lane and take the first lane on the right to reach a gate in the intake wall at Lockbank Farm.

Immediately through it, turn left and contour, passing above a wood after almost a mile. Close to where a lane climbs from the left take the steep path on your right that leads to the OS column on Winder's summit, 473 metres (1551ft) above sea level.

From now on it is all downhill. Descend, using the most southerly path which, after some 100 metres, reaches the clearly defined route to The Calf. Turn right, along it, descending steadily and eventually curving left to reach the intake wall gate used on the outward leg.

Now retrace your steps to the start.

Walk 4 - Following Kearton's Steps

Distance: **3.5 Miles (5.6 km)**

From the car park follow the B6270 briefly and bear right along a walled lane which soon crosses a valley, turns right and climbs steeply, offering a stunning view over Muker to Kisdon.

Turn right at a T-junction, along another walled lane, bridge Greenseat Beck on a packhorse bridge and, just beyond it, turn right down a steeply descending lane to a facing wall. From here, turn left, along a bridle path to a walled lane.

Once past Appletree Thwaite, continue across open fell on a clear track. Exit through a facing gate and continue close to a wall on your right to an unwalled step in it, wide enough for a gate. Go through it and continue now with the wall on your left, still on a clear track.

Bridge a wooded ghyll and follow a lane to reach the B6270. Turn right, along it, and turn left at Usha Gap Farm, directed by a 'Footpath to Muker' sign.

Bear right past the first building, then left, as directed. Continue to a stile near the second of two gates and continue over stiled fields to Muker and the car park across the bridge.

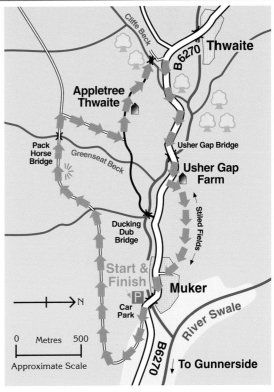

Walk 5 - A Ramble Around Reeth

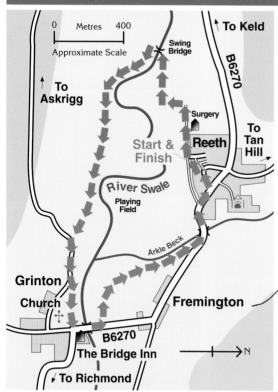

Distance: 2.5 Miles (4 km)

From the south west corner of Reeth go right between set-back houses and take a lane and follow the signs 'To the river', on the left. The path soon joins a street. Continue along it to a T-junction and go left to the road end, then right along a lane.

At the lane end, turn left, along a descending walled path, past a field house and through a gate. Continue diagonally right, soon to cross the Swale on a swing bridge.

Immediately turn left, along the river bank, and when it sweeps north, towards Reeth, keep straight ahead, soon to enter another walled path, which edges fields, then the river to reach a minor road. Here, turn left, along it, to Grinton churchyard and descend steps on the left to edge the river to Grinton.

Turn left opposite The Bridge Inn, cross Grinton Bridge, and in a short distance go left, along a path that curves right, then edges Arkle Beck to rejoin the B6270 short of it bridging Arkle Beck.

Turn left, along the road, for a return, at the end of a very pleasant and easy saunter to Reeth, hopefully refreshed by the walk and the Bridge Inn's hospitality.

Walk 6 - Inn Search of Booze

Distance: 2 Miles (3.3 km)

From the Red Lion, Langthwaite, go straight ahead, across the hamlet, leaving it eastwards, down the lane alongside Arkle Beck.

On reaching a point where a footbridge spans the beck the lane turns sharp left towards a wooded bank and curves right, through the wood, between tall trees. Where the path splits, take the left hand, upper one and, on leaving the wood continue contouring Slei Gill.

After crossing two fields go diagonally left, uphill, on a fainter path which will bring you, across steep fields, to Booze. Despite its name, Booze has no pub. Its name is Old English and means 'the house beside the curve' and the hamlet has strong Methodist links. Turn left, through Booze, along its only road which, at first, contours, giving wonderful views across the narrow valley to Calver Hill.

As the road begins its steep descent of Langthwaite Scar, it passes a viewing seat, set back from the road, for use by people with time to stop and stare. Then it is all downhill, back into Langthwaite, to celebrate in the friendly atmosphere of the Red Lion.

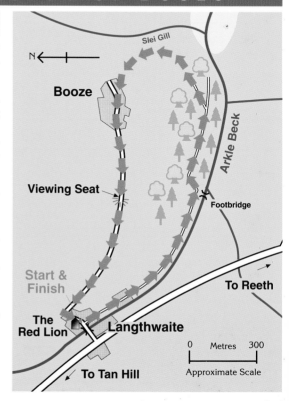

Drive 1 - A Ribblesdale Roundabout

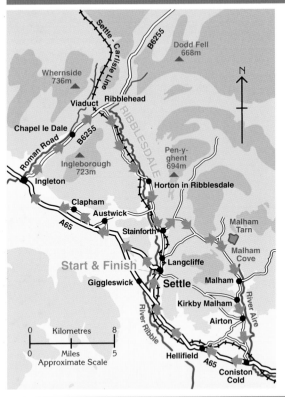

Distance: 52 Miles (84 km)

From Settle's large market square go north, cross the Ribble to join the A65, which passes Clapham, where a detour will allow you to inspect this lovely, leafy village where botanist Reginald Farrer lived in the very heart of Dalesman country. Stay on the A65 as far as the Ingleton roundabout. Turn right, along the B6255, a Roman road, driving into Three Peaks territory to Ribblehead where a famous viaduct strides across a bleak landscape.

Turn right, down Ribblesdale, passing drumlins, skirting Pen-y-ghent and visiting Horton en route to Stainforth. Turn left, through the village, soon to go right at the first road junction, through limestone uplands, taking the first left to Malham Tarn, Yorkshire's second largest lake.

From here turn right to Malham, passing breathtaking Malham Cove where a dry valley becomes a sheer cliff and forbidding Gordale Scar is just over the hill. Continue southwards, still using quiet roads, to Coniston Cold. From here, turn right, along the A65, westwards to the Settle roundabout. Turn right, back to the start. This superb circular offers so much: why 'settle' for less.

Drive 2 - O'er Vale and Dale

Distance: **49 Miles (79 km)**

From Kirkby Stephen market place take the B6259 along Mallerstang, through Nateby, past Pendragon Castle, following the course of the enchanting infant Eden. On reaching a T-junction turn left into Wensleydale, along the A684, turning left to Hardraw on approaching Hawes. Continue along the minor road to just past Hardraw and take the first left, climbing out of Wensleydale over the Buttertubs Pass into Swaledale. At a T-junction with the B6270 turn right, through Muker, following the beautiful Swale to just past Feetham. Turn left along a climbing minor road that goes behind Calver Hill and descends into Arkengarthdale near Langthwaite.

A short detour, right, to Langthwaite is most rewarding. Otherwise, go left, along this wild valley, continuing over Sleightholme Moor to Tan Hill where, at another junction, go right. After some $3^1/_2$ miles, where the road splits again, go left, then left again; descending into the Vale of Eden, passing Kaber to join the A65 and turn left, along it, for a splendid return to Kirkby Stephen. Not once is the scenery less than superb. Some car rides should not be missed. This is one of them.

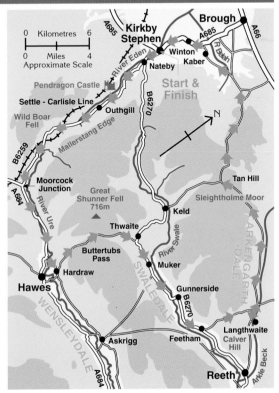

Drive 3 - An Estimable Triad

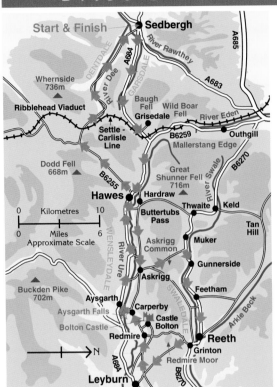

Distance: 73 Miles (118 km)

From Sedbergh take the A684 up Garsdale, passing Baugh Fell and the entrance to Grisedale, the dale that died, on the left. At Hawes, turn left to cross the Ure on a beautiful, stone bridge. On reaching a T-junction, turn right, along a quiet road to Askrigg.

Where the road splits in Askrigg, turn left and, on leaving the village, where it splits again, take the left, more direct, fork to climb over Askrigg Common and descend through spectacular countryside into Swaledale. At a T-junction, east of Muker, turn right, along the only road that runs along the valley, the B6270, going through Reeth to Grinton.

Here leave the B6270 by keeping straight ahead when the B6270 curves left, climbing out of Swaledale into Wensleydale. On descending to a cross-roads, turn right and keep straight ahead at a second cross-roads. Go through Redmire and, at the far end of Carperby, turn left to cross the Ure. Climb steeply to the A684 and go right, through Aysgarth, and on to Hawes.

Leave it, going left, along the B6255, and, after about six miles, turn right to return to Sedbergh in fine style along Dentdale.

Drive 4 - Breaking Artificial Boundaries

Distance: 65 Miles (105 km)

From Pateley Bridge take the quiet road, roughly northwards, up Nidderdale, past Gouthwaite Reservoir to Lofthouse where a short detour, left, to How Stean Gorge puts an extra cherry on the cake.

From Lofthouse a moorland road will bring you past two reservoirs, Roundhill and Leighton, to Masham, famed for the quality of the ale brewed there. When the A6108 is joined, while still in Masham, turn right, along it. Where it turns sharp right, keep straight ahead on the B6268 to a T-junction, where turn left to Bedale and take the A684 left, to Leyburn. On reaching this agricultural town, turn left, along the A6108 to cross the Ure and reach historic Middleham.

Turn right, along a minor road, past Coverham and along Coverdale to Kettlewell, the most important settlement in upper Wharfedale and a popular centre for walkers. The drive continues left, down stream, to Grassington along the B6160 from where the Wharfe is left as the route follows the B6265 over miles of wild moorland for a steep descent to Pateley Bridge where this unforgettable experience began.

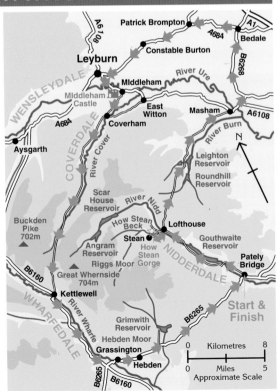

Walk 7 - An Eden Serenade

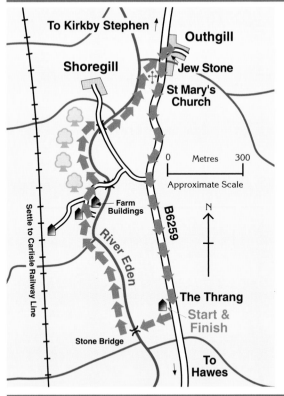

Distance: 1.5 Miles (2.5 km)

Mallerstang should be savoured like good wine, its natural beauty allowed to soak into the bones for maximum enjoyment.

From The Thrang go south, briefly, along the road, leaving through a gate on the right. Descend a bank and cross the River Eden on a beautiful stone bridge. Immediately go right, along the river bank, cross a stile in a facing wall and continue through very pleasant surroundings, following the river's gentle course. Keep on the left bank until a cluster of farm buildings is reached where a waymarker directs left between them, onto a farm road. Where it curves right to bridge the river, leave the farm road, left, cross a stile in a facing wall and go along a wooded embankment to another bridge, which cross.

Turn left, along the river's right bank on a path that leads to beautiful St Marys Church, Outhgill, which is lovingly cared for by concerned parishioners. Cut through the churchyard into Outhgill where turn left, briefly, to inspect enigmatic William Mounsey's Jew Stone. Then, hopefully having good food for thought, take the quiet road southwards to The Thrang for something to wash it down.

Walk 8 - The Kingmaker's Kingdom

Distance: 2 Miles (3.3 km)

From Middleham's lower market cross go uphill, along the road to Coverham, passing the Middleham Castle on your left. The road climbs to Middleham Low Moor, where racehorses from local stables are exercised.

Continue along this minor road which, having breasted the moor, descends gradually, with Pinker's Pond coming into view ahead as it does so. Where the wall on the left ends turn left, downhill, guided by a footpath sign, to reach the River Cover at Hullo Bridge, but do not cross it.

Instead, cross a stile on your left and follow the left bank, climbing above it. Edge a large field to its far corner, where turn left, soon to edge a plantation on your right. Cross a stile near its end and follow a clear path through the pines to exit in a large pasture, having simply cut off the plantation's corner.

Go right, across the pasture aiming for a point at its far boundary where the wall becomes a fence. Here turn left, uphill, passing a waymarker, cross a stile and another field to enter a lane through a gate. This descending lane will return you past Middleham Castle back to the start of this lovely walk.

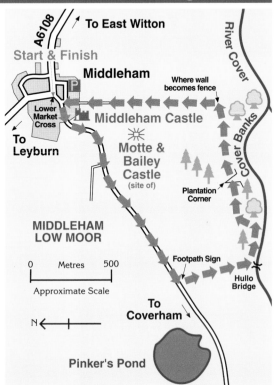

Walk 9 - Hardraw's Stylish Stile Saunter

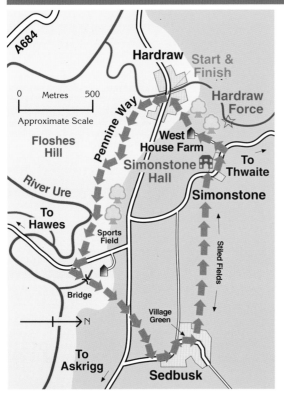

Distance: 2.5 Miles (4 km)

Leave Hardraw, southwards, alongside the beck on your right, guided by a 'Pennine Way' sign, soon to bear left along a flagged path. Cross the next four fields on this path, then go diagonally right to cross a stile in a wall on your right.

Immediately turn left, close to the wall and, where it ends, continue ahead to cross a stile in a facing wall. Go diagonally right over a sports field to a road. Turn right, along it, and, where it curves right, go left over a signposted stile.

Bear left along a field path, cross a bridge, climb a bank and cross to the right hand corner of the next field. Continue over the road ahead, diagonally right, cross a stile and take the right hand path over fields to the Sedbusk road. Turn left, along it, to the village green.

Leave left, midway along it, at a stile signposted 'Simonside'. Cross a succession of stiled fields to a road. Just past Simonstone Hall go left, as signposted, then through an avenue of trees to descend to West House Farm. Turn right at a footpath sign and descend to Hardraw, seen ahead.

Walk 10 - Ure A Sweetheart!

Distance: 2.5 Miles (4 km)

Ure a real honey! and you start at The Falls Country Club with these directions:

Take the steep road downhill, cross the Ure just below High Falls and stay on the road, first alongside the river, then climbing away from it to the first junction on the right.

From here turn right, along a lane. After half a mile it curves right, continuing as a farm road for a further half mile to Hollins House Farm.

Go left, passing the farm house, as waymarked, go through a gate on your left into a field and follow a clear path down another field. Where it curves left, keep ahead, cross a signposted stile and continue alongside a fence to a 'Footpath to Castle Bolton' sign. Here turn left, descend to a riverside path and follow it upstream, passing Aysgarth's Lower and Middle Falls.

On regaining the road continue along it, re-cross the Ure and climb steps ahead to St Andrew's Church, exiting the churchyard uphill to the A684, where turn right, briefly, and right again to descend to The Falls Country Club.

Yes, Ure a sweetheart. I could fall, fall, fall for you!

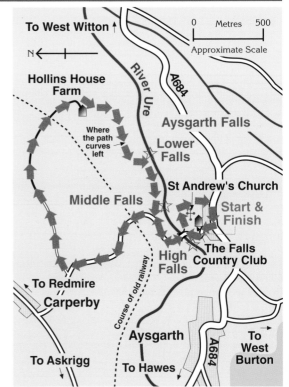

Walk 11 - A Pen-y-ghent Ascent

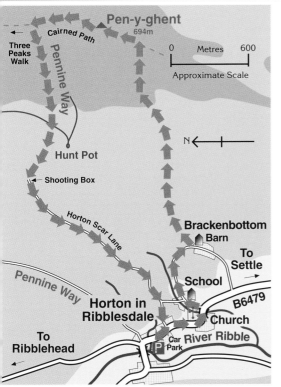

Distance: 5 Miles (8 km)

Leave Horton car park turning right, through the village, past the church and over Horton Bridge, turn left and take the road alongside the beck on your left to Brackenbottom.

Just short of a barn on your left go through two gates and climb the field ahead, exiting over a stile.

The route climbs, close to a wall on the right, to a facing stile, continues climbing towards Pen-y-ghent, seen ahead, first to a facing gateway, then to two stiles to reach the bottom of Pen-y-ghent's snout.

Here begins the steep climb to the summit, first up well worn rocks, then, nearer the broad top, along duckboards, which please use because of erosion difficulties.

Leave the summit over a ladder stile and follow a well cairned track that gradually descends the western scarp to a junction of paths, where go left, along a track so clear that a blind man couldn't miss it.

When Horton Scar Lane is reached, go left, along it, back to Horton car park, ready for a well deserved pint of milk or the like; and you know who supplies that.

Walk 12 - Elgar's Land of Hope & Glory

Distance: 3.5 Miles (5.6 km)

Fall in love with Settle scenery as Elgar did. Here's how. From Settle Market Place use the pedestrian crossing and keep straight ahead, going under a viaduct and continuing to just before the Fire Station where go left, along a road that soon curves right, past a mill, to bridge the Ribble. Turn right, along the riverside, to Settle Bridge, cross the main road and follow a signposted path to Stackhouse.

Turn right, along a minor road, and, immediately past a white fronted house on the right, turn right to the river, which bridge and take a lane to the B6479. Turn right, along it, for a short distance to reach Langcliffe, where turn left, through the village along a tarmac road that climbs through a gateway.

Here cross a stile on your right, go up the hillside and, where the wall on your right turns right, do likewise. Continue close to the wall on your right, crossing stiles, along a clear, green path which becomes a track, descending into Settle. Where it reaches a surfaced road, continue straight ahead and where it divides, turn left and continue to Settle Market Place.

Did you good, didn't it. Nothing enigmatic about this walk.

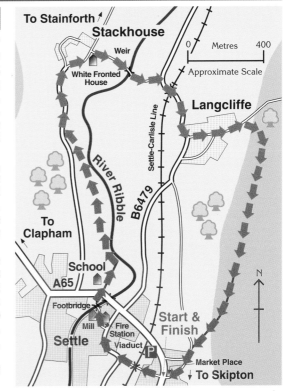

The Cart House
Hardraw, near Hawes

Some things wrinkle with age, but The Cart House is not one of them. It has mellowed and looks younger in age than it did when young. Although it is more than one hundred years old it never got a telegram from the Queen! - perhaps someone forgot to tell her. But it did get a face lift in 1983 when the original farm building was converted into today's family run tea room and craft shop. As befits such a building it is run with loving care by members of a long established farming household.

Now, if any folk know about satisfying the inner man with good, wholesome fare it is farming folk; and in the tea room a great deal of care is taken to ensure that only wholesome food is available. In particular the soups and the cakes are extremely good. They are all made on the premises and whenever possible organic ingredients are used for you to devour in pleasant, clean surroundings.

In the days before World War II at hirings in farming areas like Hardraw, when the wage offered was pretty much the same from farm to farm, the deciding factor, before the prospective hand accepted the job, was whether or not the farm was 'a good grub shop'. Well, The Cart House, by any standards, is a good grub shop.

The soups are home-made, as is the wholemeal bread and the salads are crisp and fresh and richly flavoured, good to look at and even better to taste. The flat, open tarts are

'flantasic', the fruit cakes really fruity and the sandwiches, with various fillings, are seasoned with mouth watering goodness.

The local Wensleydale cheeses are as fresh and exciting as the new recipes from which they are made. And to wash them down there are fruit juices, milk shakes, milk, coffee or tea.

A most pleasing adjunct to the tea room is the work of a local artist and photographer displayed there. It is a nice touch, the result of careful thought given to the wellbeing of the customer by Clara and Mavis Fawcett, who really do care about their visitors.

The Cart House is open seven days a week from 10am until 5.30pm during the months of March to November inclusive with a really good choice of food available throughout the day.

The same high standard of care that is taken to ensure that only real, wholesome food is available in the tea room applies to the gift shop where every attempt is made to ensure that browsing there is a pleasurable experience. The items for sale are chosen for their quality and interest and many of them are available nowhere else in the area.

Nearby, magnificent Hardraw Force plunges into a natural amphitheatre where, on a tightrope, Blondin once fried eggs. Unfortunately, no one had told him about the many delights of The Cart House.

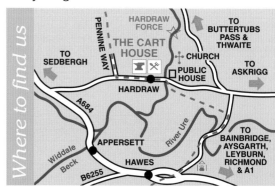

For further information, contact:

**THE CART HOUSE,
HARDRAW, NR HAWES,
NORTH YORKSHIRE,
DL8 3LZ
TEL: 0969 667691**

The Bridge Inn
Grinton-in-Swaledale

Grinton has always been rather special. Its splendid mother church of St Andrew, with its churchyard, is known as the cathedral of the dales; and all Swaledale upstream of the hamlet is its parish. Before a new chapel and burial ground were consecrated at Muker, in 1580, all the burials in the parish were at Grinton. After that date the deceased from upper Swaledale, above Gunnerside, were buried at Muker while those below Gunnerside continued to be buried at Grinton, being carried there in rough, wicker baskets, on men's shoulders. The route taken was known as the Corpse Way, although it was not used exclusively for that purpose.

If churches were women, St Andrew's would be a well upholstered matron, getting on a bit but holding her age well. The oldest parts are Norman, dating from the C12th and much of the chancel arch is C13th, as is the richly moulded porch archway. The worshippers, however, belong to the C20th; and St Andrew's bridges this gap nicely. The hymn books are Ancient and Modern.

The two centres around which the social life of Grinton revolves are St Andrew's and the nearby Bridge Inn. Nothing of importance that happens around Grinton goes unobserved and without comment by either or both of these two admirable establishments. Together, they are the fingers on the pulse of local life and sometimes they poke about a bit and unearth some juicy morsel of local interest.

Originally built as a farm in 1630, the Bridge Inn was granted a drover's licence in 1671 and obtained a full licence in 1675. The building has grown somewhat and now incorporates the original farm, an adjoining cottage, built in 1610, and a stable, all of which blend in warm mellowness.

Inside Trevor and Margaret Hird will be delighted to see to your needs. During the summer months they are open from 11am until 11pm, in winter from noon until 3pm and from 6pm until 11pm. Throughout the year Sunday opening is from noon until 3pm and from 7pm until 10.30pm. At other times the Law takes possession. They are a local family from nearby Reeth and, being Swaledale folk, have an inbuilt sense of integrity, service and dependability, all flavoured with hearty dales humour.

This is a real ale inn and the choice includes Black Sheep bitter, Theakston's brews, including Old Peculiar, John Smith's best bitter and Magnet. If you don't give a Four X for beer, the lagers include Fosters, Murphey's stout is on tap and scrumpy is available.

As well as the main bar there is a games room and a lounge diner. One hundred people can be seated inside with a further forty outside.

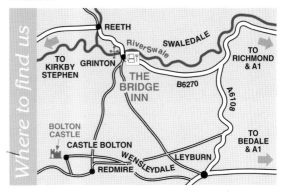

Meals are available throughout all opening times with home-made specialities like steak and kidney pie and prime sirloin in Old Peculiar great favourites with the many regulars.

Hikers are always welcome at the Bridge Inn which, being at the very heart of beautiful Swaledale, is a welcome haven at the end of many a strenuous slog in this 'land of rest'.

For further information, contact:

**THE BRIDGE INN,
GRINTON-IN-SWALEDALE,
RICHMOND, NORTH YORKSHIRE,
DL11 6HH
TEL: 0748 84224**

The Kings Arms
Redmire

The Kings Arms has long been a loyal name; but times change and whereas the arms of King Charles II were filled with Nell Gwynne, Redmire's Kings Arms is filled with good food, good beer and good sandwiches! This remarkable achievement has been recorded in trade guides for the past seven years and endorsed by many good, discerning folk, who habitually aim for the Kings Arms when in need of sustenance, relaxation and a friendly atmosphere.

The Kings Arms is all that a country pub should be. Nestling in the charming village of Redmire, with its quaint cottages and houses set around several pretty greens from where enchanted footpaths explore broad, mellow and restful Wensleydale, seeking out jewels in the vale's rich tapestry like the splendid Redmire Falls, it attracts the discriminating like bears to honey.

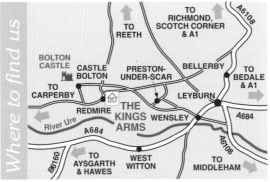

The high regard in which the Kings Arms is held in the hearts of the regulars is a direct result of the hard work and devotion put into it by Roger and Tracy Stevens who, with their son, Nigel, and daughter, Vicky, ensure that all their customers are cared for most handsomely. Nothing is too much trouble; and it pays off as 'family fun' becomes the order of the day.

Your preferred order of the day may be hand pulled real ale like John Smiths and Theakstons Best with Tetleys, Theakstons XB and Websters all available along with 53 malt whiskies and good Rombouts coffee; and repeat orders are always on tap.

The neatly kept and simply furnished bar has a relaxed and unassuming atmosphere. A long soft leatherette wall seat and other upholstered settles adorn the bar along with red leatherette cafe chairs set about round cast iron tables where you can play footsie if the mood takes you; or you can sit in a fine oak

armchair if it doesn't! It is all so relaxed: and a wood-burning stove enhances this friendliness.

Many of the interesting photos adorning the walls are of local filming for 'All Creatures Great and Small'.

Roger and Vicky do most of the excellent cooking for the Inn's restaurant with such delights as Chicken specialities, grilled local Trout and Duck. Popular bar meals, all home-cooked, include soup, excellent pate in a lovely brown terrine pot, very good omelettes or steak and kidney pie, to name but a few.

If you dare, finish off your meal with one of the 'wicked' puddings. An old fashioned pie or crumble or perhaps Death by Chocolate or Chocolate Roulade.

There is accommodation in just two quiet, double rooms, both with washbasin, colour TV and tea-making equipment.

Nowhere has better views than the panoramic scene from the patio, on the inn's south side. The views across Wensleydale to Pen Hill are superb. There are chairs and tables in the pretty garden, an ideal setting in which to enjoy a drink or a snack.

If you prefer there are darts, pool, dominoes, pub quizzes and 'sing alongs'. Once, an apocryphal tale goes; someone staggered from the Kings Arms clutching a pint. He stumbled under a tree and spilled his drink. Today that tree has to be propped up!

For further information, contact:

**THE KINGS ARMS,
REDMIRE, LEYBURN,
NORTH YORKSHIRE,
DL8 4ED
TEL: 0969 22316**

How Stean Gorge & Cafe
Lofthouse

Anyone holding fading memories of the Grimalewald in Switzerland who takes the scenic road northwards from Gouthwaite Reservoir, past Ramsgill, can be forgiven for becoming disorientated, of thinking him or her self conveyed, as on a magic carpet, back to that glorious place: for the likeness is uncanny enough to have earned this exciting limestone area the sobriquet 'Yorkshire's little Switzerland'.

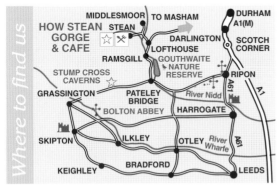

Where to find us

As though to allay doubts about the limestone, before the road enters Lofthouse it bridges the dry bed of the Nidd, the water having gone underground. Do not take this as a personal affront: the river is responding to the nature of the bedrock, not your presence.

The road bifurcates in Lofthouse, the right fork going past ancient cottages and farms, climbing steeply on its way to Masham. The left one splits again, right to terminate at Middlesmoor and left, over How Stean Beck, to Stean where it ends.

Stean Moor, spreading upwards and westwards from Stean is both birthplace and nursery to the precocious How Stean Beck, a milk churn of froth and gurgles as it tumbles from the heights; tossing and turning in its limestone bed. How Stean Gorge, which the road to Stean skirts, shows the beck at its most spectacular. For here rushing waters surge past huge boulders and glide over deep pools where fat trout lie, along the narrow confines of a dramatic ravine, formed during the Ice Age and, in places, 80 feet deep.

Howard Stevenson is keeper of the Gorge, charged with seeing that it does not get lost! This is not as easy as it would at first appear to be for, in springtime, it is smothered in wild flowers, clusters of primroses, great drifts of daffodils and congestions of bluebells. Furthermore, birds flock there; yellow hammers, dippers, blackbirds, woodpeckers

and many others of the same genus flitter and twitter about the gorge bringing colour and song.

Mellow autumn brings spectacular sunsets to How Stean Gorge and as the days shorten and playful winds bowl along crinkly curls of colourful leaves and mist fills the hollows, icicles grow on limestone overhangs and gossamer spiders' webs sparkle like pearls in the crisp air.

Winter is a study in black and white.

How Stean Gorge is open daily from 10am until sunset.

The cafe is open daily, except Mondays and Tuesdays during January and February and Christmas Day, with a day menu between 10am and 6pm and, during the summer months, an evening menu between 6pm and last orders at 8pm.

The traditional 'Sunday lunches', which are served daily, are home-cooked and Howard's specialities, especially his bilberry pie, are a must. All the cakes served at afternoon tea, are home-made and taste delicious, and, yes, there is a table licence with all the meals. So go on, gorge yourself!

Coniston Hall Estate
Coniston Cold, Skipton in Craven

The Coniston Hall Estate is situated to the west of Gargrave on the A65, the Gargrave to Hellifield road. Its tea-rooms are open daily for morning coffee, lunch, afternoon teas and high teas. Private hire and party facilities are available and coach parties are made very welcome at Coniston Hall Estate, and this, together with its convenient location, makes it an ideal stop-over for those wishing to explore Airedale and Ribblesdale.

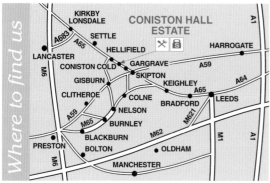

The Coniston Hall Estate is set in the extensive sheep farming area of Craven. In a Poll Tax survey dated 1379 a fulling mill is recorded as being in operation at Coniston Cold. It was an essential process in woollen manufacture and was the next stage after the weaving of the web. The first fulling mills were established close to cloth making centres and one fuller could serve many weavers.

Coniston Cold has a strong Lancashire connection through the manufacture of cotton. The combined attractions of a watercourse with a flow strong enough to drive a water wheel and nearness to good canal and road access by way of Skipton attracted Lancashire's cotton barons to the Yorkshire Dales. Cotton spinning water-mills were established at several places in Craven, including one at Coniston Cold.

The Pennine Way passes close to Coniston Hall Estate on its way northwards from Gargrave to Airton, Malham and some of the finest limestone countryside in England.

Malham, one of the honeypots of the Dales, at the head of Malhamdale, is only a short car drive away from Coniston Hall Estates. A quiet road northwards from Coniston Cold through Bele Busk and five miles beyond it will bring you nicely to this village, which straddles the beck flowing from the base of dramatic Malham Scar. Hereabouts, the limestone countryside can be seen in all its breathtaking magnificence.

Goredale Scar, where water pours into a dark chasm overhung with tall cliffs, Janet's Foss, a little downstream, Malham Tarn, which would not exist without its Silurian Slate bed, the spectacular dry river bed below it and the famous pavement on top of Malham Scar, all close together, will fill a day with interest and whet an appetite that Coniston Hall Estate will be happy to satisfy.

Should you wish to take home some of the flavour of this lovely area the Estate shop may be able to help. It is open seven days a week and fresh trout and fine country produce can be purchased there, where helpful staff are on hand to help. There is also a wide range of smoked fish from the Estate Smokehouse, meats and poultry.

A picturesque 24 acre lake and 2½ miles of double-bank fly fishing on the River Aire have filled many an angler's day with contentment; and the old magic is still there. However, should your inclination be more towards shooting, Coniston Hall Estate can offer first class clay pigeon shooting facilities from the beginner to the expert.

For children there is an adventure playground.

The South Craven Fault line is evident at Buckham Brow, near Settle. Coniston Hall Estate is without blemish.

For further information, contact:

**CONISTON HALL ESTATE,
CONISTON COLD,
SKIPTON IN CRAVEN,
NORTH YORKSHIRE, BD23 4EB
TEL: 0756 748136 FAX: 0756 749551**

Durants
Middleham

Middleham, spread along the hillside in Lower Wensleydale between the rivers Ure and Cover, is a place with a glorious past involving a king maker and a king and a bright today built on the sport of kings.

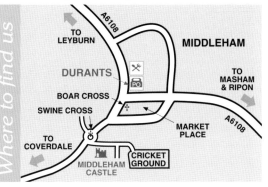

'The King Maker' was Richard, Earl of Warwick, greatest of the powerful almost royal Neville family, whose home was Middleham Castle during its most glorious years. Following his death, the castle was forfeited to the Crown. Edward IV gave it to his brother Richard, Duke of York, who became Richard III and married Warwick's daughter, so returning the castle to the Neville family. All good, historical stuff kept on the boil by the Fellowship of the White Boar and the long shot of finding another religious bijou, valued at £1.3 million, while on one of the many superb local walks.

Middleham boasts two crosses, the Swine Cross and near its centre, the Boar Cross, close to where stands an imposing, stone built building, erected during the Napoleonic Wars. It is called Durants and here Tony and Judy Ward, assisted by their friendly, helpful staff, make a good job of seeing to the varied needs of locals and visitors alike every day of the week between 9am and 5pm.

They run a post office and general store on the ground floor, which fronts, upstairs, the largest art gallery in the dales where gifts, books and maps are on tempting display. Just the place for picking up a bargain; and it won't cost you a mint of Monet!

Durants' thick walls also hide a tearoom and a coffee lounge where all manner of good, home-made, Yorkshire fare is available, including 'Fat Rascals', treacle tarts and curd tarts, all specialities, freshly made and delicious. If you fancy something different, on offer are a mean ploughmans' lunch served with local, Richard III, Wensleydale cheese,

chicken and ham and other equally tempting pies along with home-made soups that really haven't seen the inside of a tin. You can smell the difference, tell the difference, and it shows. To aid digestion try Durants' speciality teas, coffee or soft drinks.

Middleham has been a famous horse breeding and training centre for centuries. Ever since Isaac Cape of Tupgill became the first professional trainer, circa 1765, Middleham and horseracing have been synonymous. Until 1872 there was a racecourse on Middleham Moor. Today trainers rent common land on High Moor, Low Moor and Busks Pasture, which provide splendid gallops for some 300 locally trained horses, among them some possible Grand National and Derby winners like locally trained 'Sheila's Cottage', 'Teal' and 'Dante'.

Distinguished owner Neville Crump was firmly established in Middleham in 1948 when his long shot, 'Sheila's Cottage', won the National by a neck at 50 to 1, causing him to smack her on the rump with an endearing, "Well done! you old bitch!"

This is worth remembering when eating Durants 'Fat Rascals', because the person who makes these mouth watering treats is Tony, not Judy. Forewarned is forearmed.

For further information, contact:

**DURANTS,
MARKET PLACE, MIDDLEHAM,
NORTH YORKSHIRE,
DL8 4PE
TEL: 0969 23251**

The Posthorn
Sedbergh

The general consensus is that the cartographer was not thinking clearly when he stuck Sedbergh in Yorkshire. It is in Cumbria, where it belongs; but it is included here to propitiate those myriad people who still fervently believe that Dentdale and Garsdale, with Sedbergh at their feet, are the finest of the Yorkshire Dales. The more unlikely the fabrication, the more likely it will be believed. The cartographer would not have become inebriated in the first place if he had had the gumption to first line his stomach with a feast of Yorkshire ham and eggs at the Posthorn. But he didn't and, in fairness, he couldn't because the Posthorn was not the Posthorn then, it was the Kings Arms, a coaching inn. There, at 7.30 each morning, the 'Lord Exmouth' stopped to change horses and for passengers to receive welcome nourishment on their journey from Lancaster to Newcastle.

During the early days of coaching, circa 1750, the cost of travel was generally cheaper in the north of England than in the south but the standard of service varied considerably from coaching inn to coaching inn. The Old Kings Arms at Leeds was dirty and disagreeable while the New Inn at Castle Howard was an excellent house but dirty and the landlady was saucy! In Kendal, the Kings Arms was a good house, very civil and remarkably cheap, with a brace of woodcock, veal cutlets and cheese at 1/- a head. The Kings Arms in Sedbergh, I suspect, was on a par with its Kendal namesake. At any rate there is no doubt about its rating today, as the Posthorn. It is first class.

True, the price of tea and coffee is up on the 6d a head it cost 250 years ago; but greater variety compensates for that. The Posthorn serves a large selection of teas and coffees from all over the world along with something rather special you would not find in coaching days, herb and fruit teas.

The Posthorn, which has seating for 50, is open seven days a week from 9am until 5.30pm. It overlooks the market square and the church, so, if you have a 'Keyhole Kate' personality, should you be a nosey devil, you can survey the passing throng over a tea or coffee, a snack, lunch, afternoon tea or, on Sundays, succulent roast beef and Yorkshire pudding. And here's a novelty: a real hearty, dales breakfast; just the job for a martyr about to climb Winder.

Sedbergh is an ideal base from which to walk that magnificent triangle of rounded fells, the Howgills that lie like slumbering elephants between the Lake District proper and the Pennines. Nestling at a meeting point of dales, where roads from north and south Westmorland meet routes from Yorkshire and Lancashire, it is only 30 minutes away from the Lake District National Park by car.

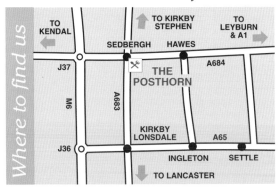

Alan and Chris Clowes are the proprietors of this estimable establishment. Chris is usually behind the scenes, preparing the food in the kitchen; but Alan is much in evidence, usually chatting with the customers while Janet, the senior waitress, flits hither and thither, carrying things. Oh! what a jolly lot! I must make another visit.

For further information, contact:

**THE POSTHORN,
30 MAIN STREET,
SEDBERGH,
CUMBRIA, LA10 5BL
TEL: 05396 21389**

Pen-y-ghent Cafe
Horton-in-Ribblesdale

Pen-y-ghent Cafe is not a walkers' cafe it is THE walkers' cafe. The welfare of those hardy (sometimes foolhardy) backpackers and the needs of the car borne walkers just wishing to enjoy the outdoors in more leisurely fashion is the main reason for its existence and has been since the Bayes family settled there some twenty-eight years ago.

An example of their understanding of the special needs of the walking fraternity is the unique clock card booking out system based on an old factory time clock. This system operates daily except for Tuesdays and Fridays and can be a life saver. The procedure is straight forward but extremely effective. Anyone tackling the gruelling 26 mile circuit of Yorkshire's Three Peaks or other local walks is welcome to fill out a clock card entering their name, home address telephone number, car registration, and where parked.

The departure time is imprinted by punching the time clock at the start of the walk and the card is retained at the cafe until the walker returns.

More importantly, should the wanderer fail to return at the heel of the day the card will show this and even when the cafe is closed the system remains in operation, with food and drink being available to the late returner.

If one is alarmingly overdue the emergency services are alerted. The system is also used by cavers and potholers.

No other cafe I know operates a safety system like the one at Pen-y-ghent Cafe and this is why among the walking and caving fraternities its reputation is sky high.

To become eligible for invitation to membership of the Three Peaks of Yorkshire

Club the circuit must be completed within the traditional 12 hours.

Pen-y-ghent looming over the village is perhaps the most popular local walk. The 5-mile circular which takes about three hours is eminently suitable for families with young children.

A special visitors book for Pennine Way walkers supported by a display of log sheets sent in by Pennine Wayfarers makes interesting reading. Both are well thumbed because people like to know in whose steps they trod.

The fare includes a menu embracing a variety of sustaining foods and huge mugs of hot drinks for all outdoor enthusiasts. There are no table cloths to soil, no worries about muddy boots or wet steaming cagoules, and even people in polished shoes who arrive by car or coach are welcome.

The adjoining outdoor shop offers many essentials from the humble can-opener to quality protective walking gear, along with footcare products and Kendal Mint Cake - in short, 'everything but the walker'.

Guide books and maps in profusion adorn the entrance area which also doubles as the English Tourist Board officially networked Horton-in-Ribblesdale Tourist Information Centre. As well as dealing with personal callers, a local bed booking service is operated.

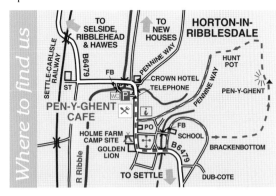

For further information, contact:

**PEN-Y-GHENT CAFE,
HORTON-IN-RIBBLESDALE,
SETTLE, NORTH YORKSHIRE,
BD24 0HE
TEL: 0729 860333 FAX: 0729 860333**

Country Style
Settle

If you had a reading room with an interesting cast iron pillar supporting the structure and it was in Bishopdale Court, which is reputed to be the oldest thoroughfare in Settle, what would you do with it? Norman and Maureen Robson built a family business around it, called Country Style, because that's what it has. Engaging some friendly part time staff and opened it seven days a week for morning coffee and light lunches. That's how it started.

The coffee is rather exotic, coming, as it does, from a manufacturer so rich his house stands in its own grounds, the potatoes modestly remain jacketed, vegetarians drool over the salads while people like myself, only half inclined in that direction, who, for the most part, tend to eat only meat from animals that eat grass, can tackle the quiches and anything else on offer with impunity.

Still waters run deep, hiding undercurrents, and Country Style, it must be said, is not without a tincture of covert contention. It is all Maureen's fault. She thinks her famous carrot cake is tastier than the carrot cake Sarah makes! It's enough to make you want to echo Bugs Bunny's 'What's up doc?' So be diplomatic: order one of each and, if asked to judge, zip your lip!

The Paradise flan cake is a little bit of Heaven and 'A Little Bit of Heaven' is cosmic. The date and cherry cake is also out of this world and a slice of apricot and cinnamon will spice your day.

Country Style is open seven days a week from 10 o'clock in the morning, except Sunday when it opens at 10.30am; and just in case you can't remember what day it is Country Style will keep you right!

Tuesday is Market Gossip Day when the conversation goes like this: 'Eh, our Liz has had her face lifted'.

'Go on! They'll pinch anything these days'!

The original idea was to hang local artists in the Coffee Shop, but it was discarded as being unhygenic and unsightly! A compromise was reached and now their varied and excellent paintings grace the coffee shop walls.

Country Style does a fine line in pine. It is beautiful furniture and reasonably priced, all part of the country image and all good quality. Other country collectables, like the selection of baskets, are on display and are good buys.

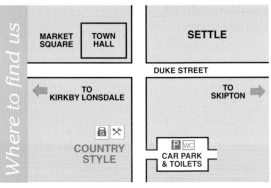

Where to find us

MARKET SQUARE | TOWN HALL | SETTLE

DUKE STREET

TO KIRKBY LONSDALE | TO SKIPTON

COUNTRY STYLE | CAR PARK & TOILETS

Limestone Cliffs overlook this bustling market town at the southern end of the famous Settle to Carlisle line, the most scenic railway in England. Unfortunately, more than a hundred lives were lost during its construction and twenty viaducts and fourteen tunnels are found along its route.

The Elgar Way links places around Settle and is super to walk. Why not try it. Do it in style, Country Style.

For further information, contact:

**COUNTRY STYLE,
BISHOPDALE COURT,
SETTLE, NORTH YORKSHIRE,
BD24 9EB
TEL: 05242 62941**